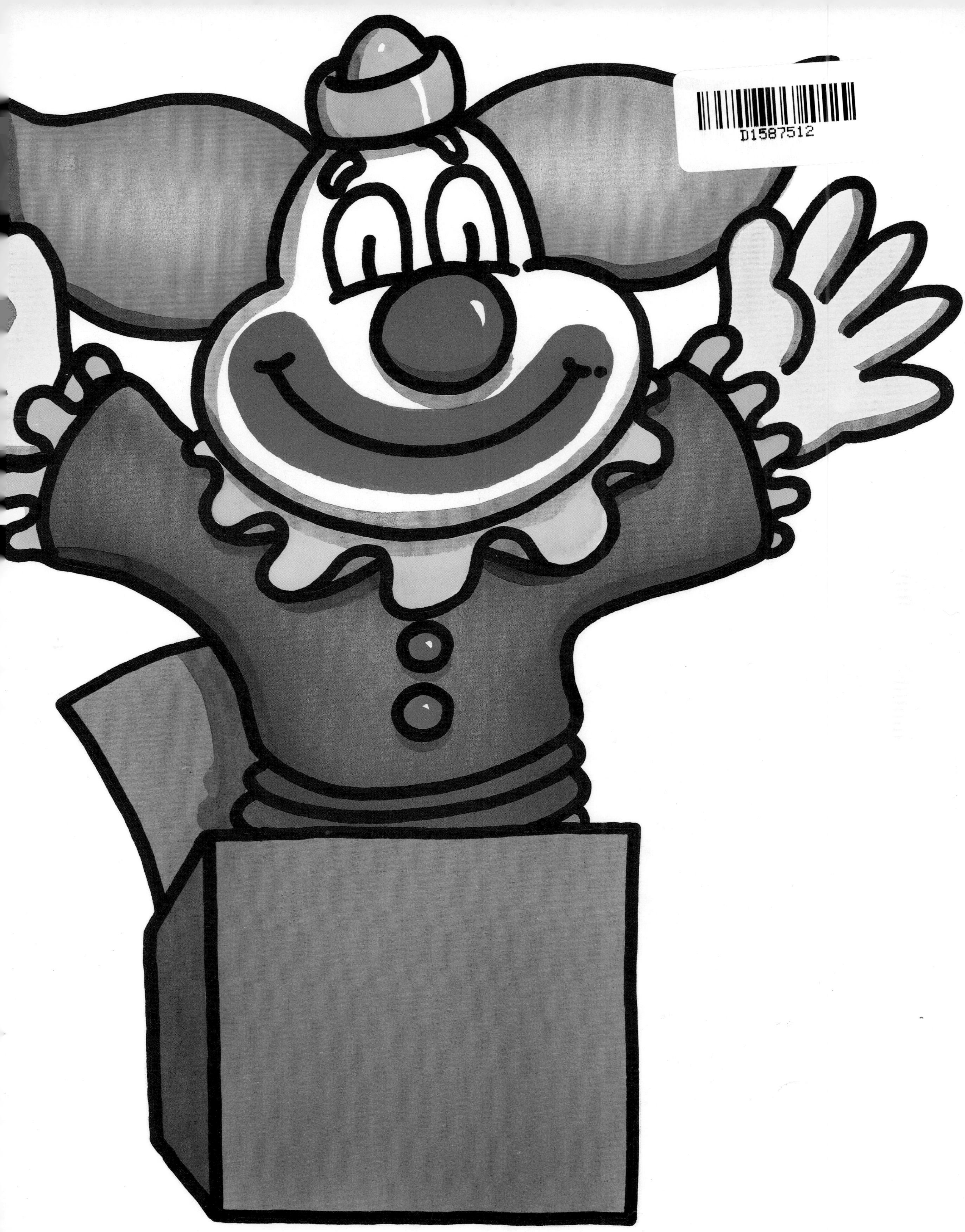

CIRCLE

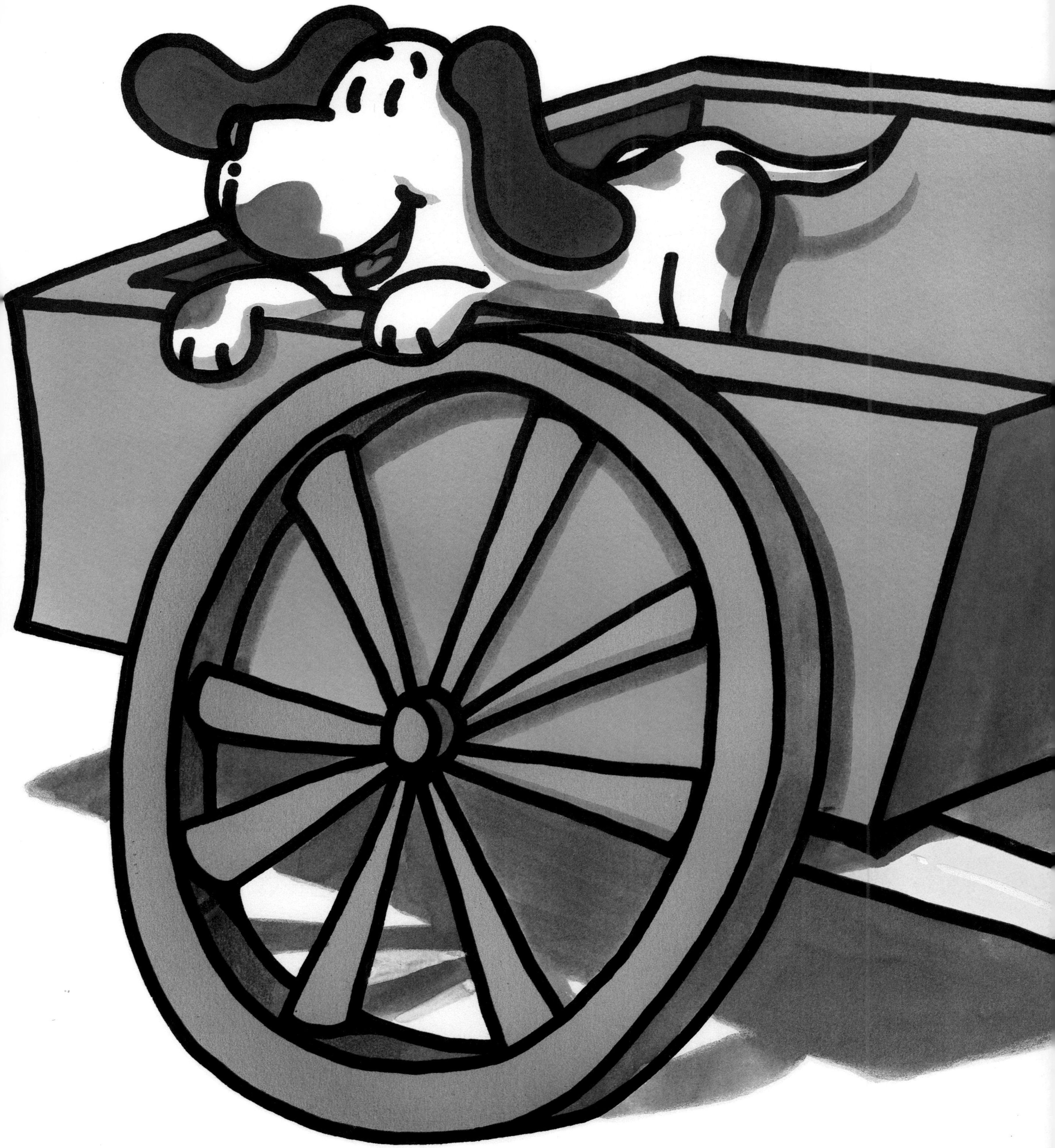

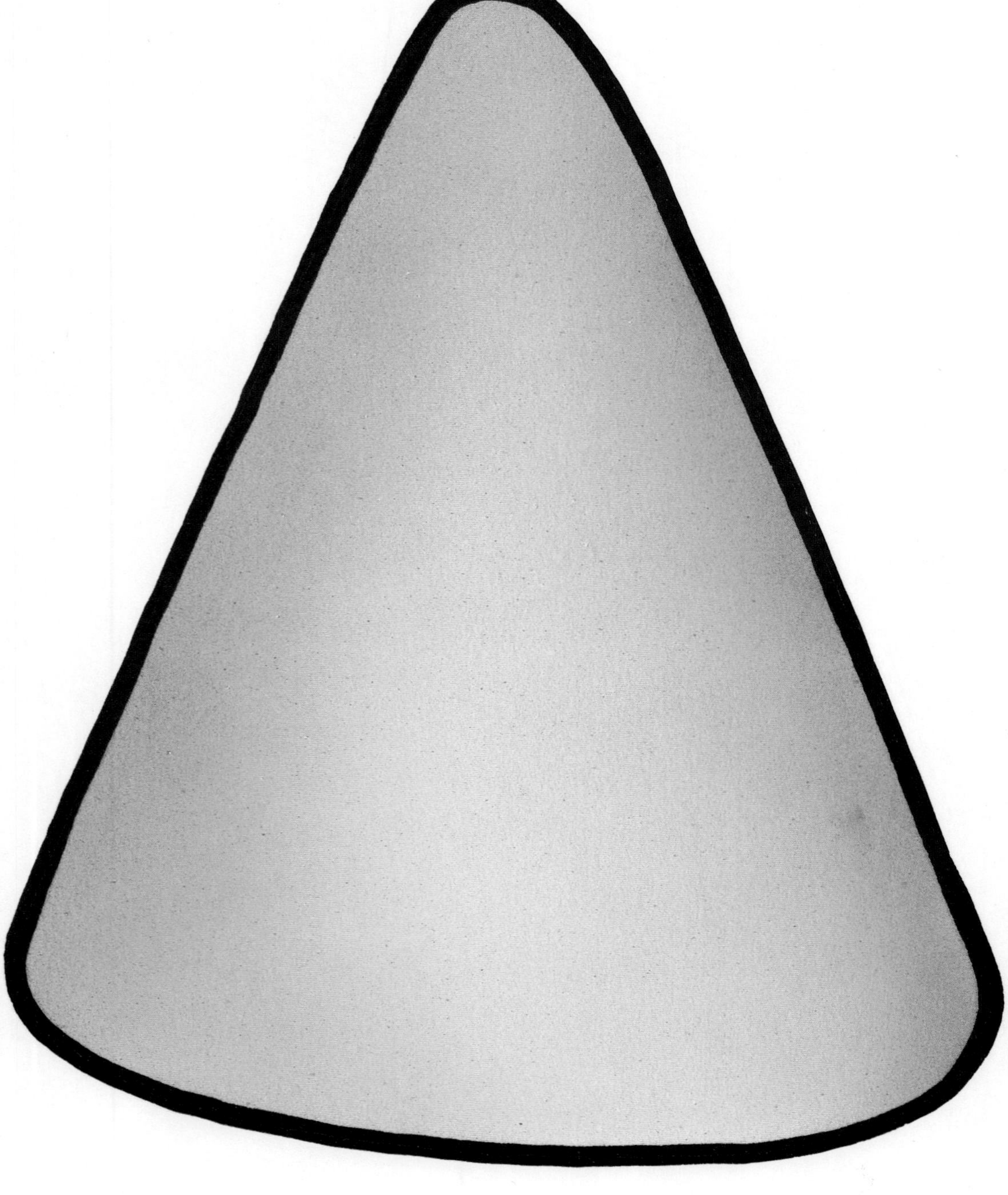

CONE

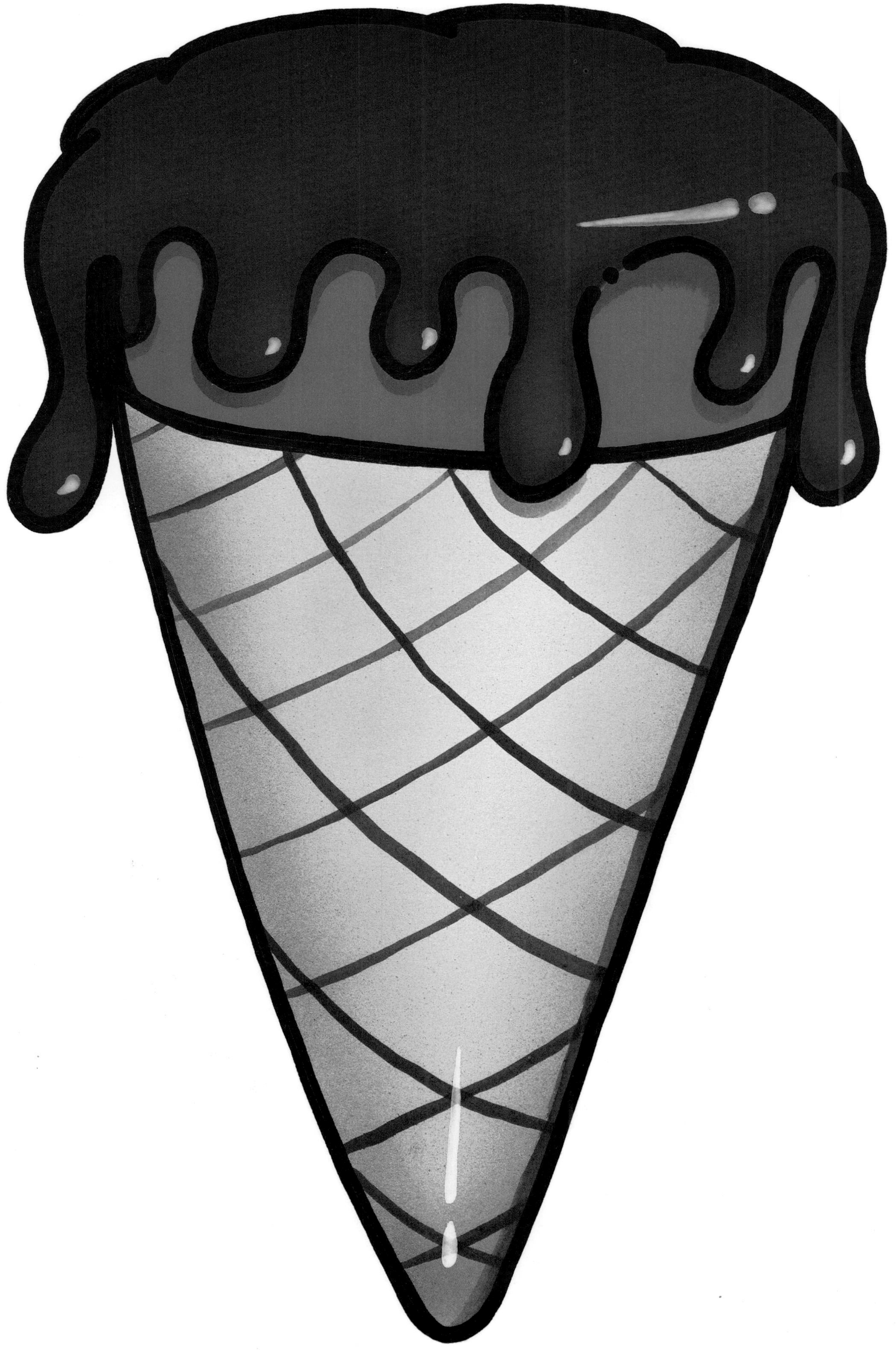

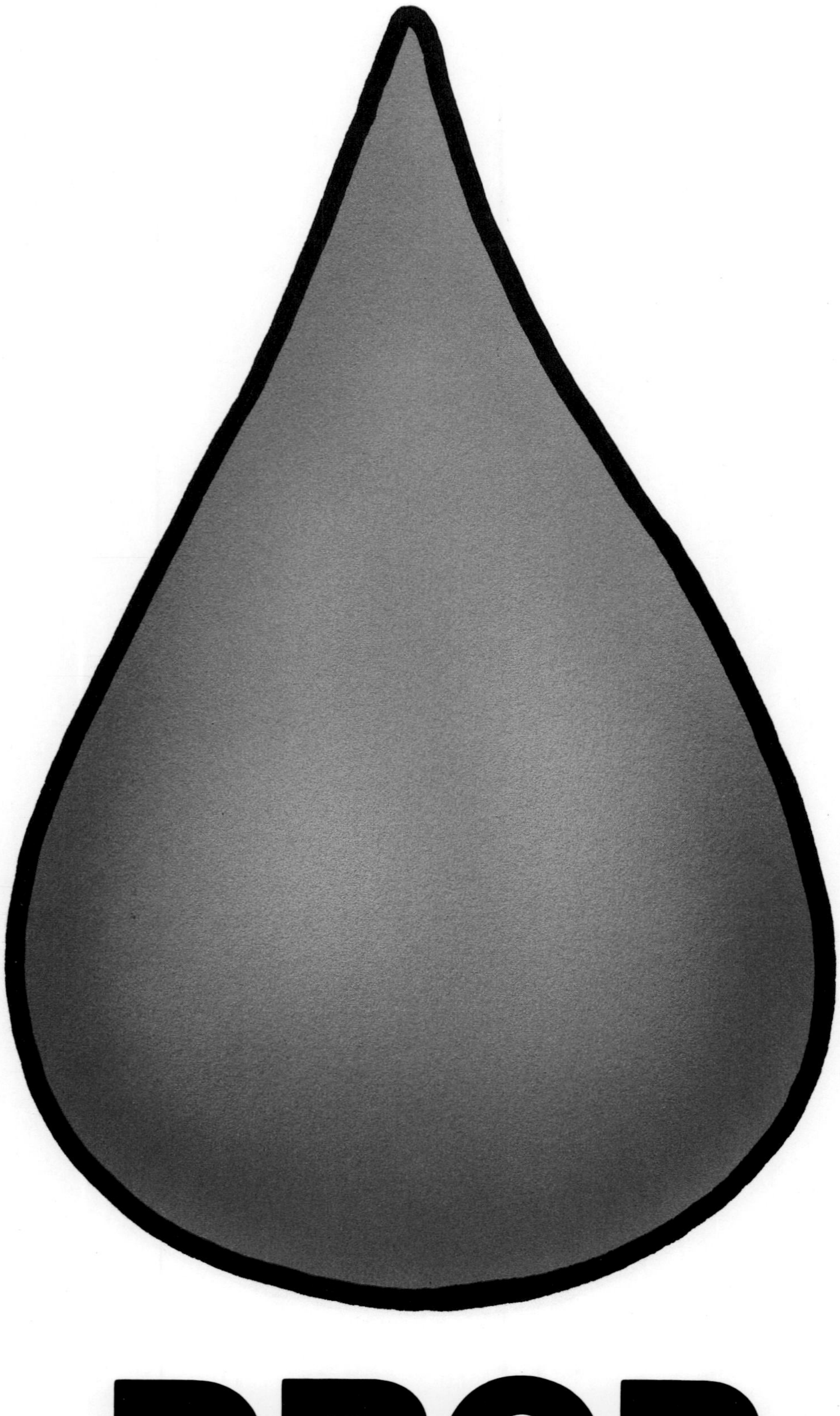

DROP

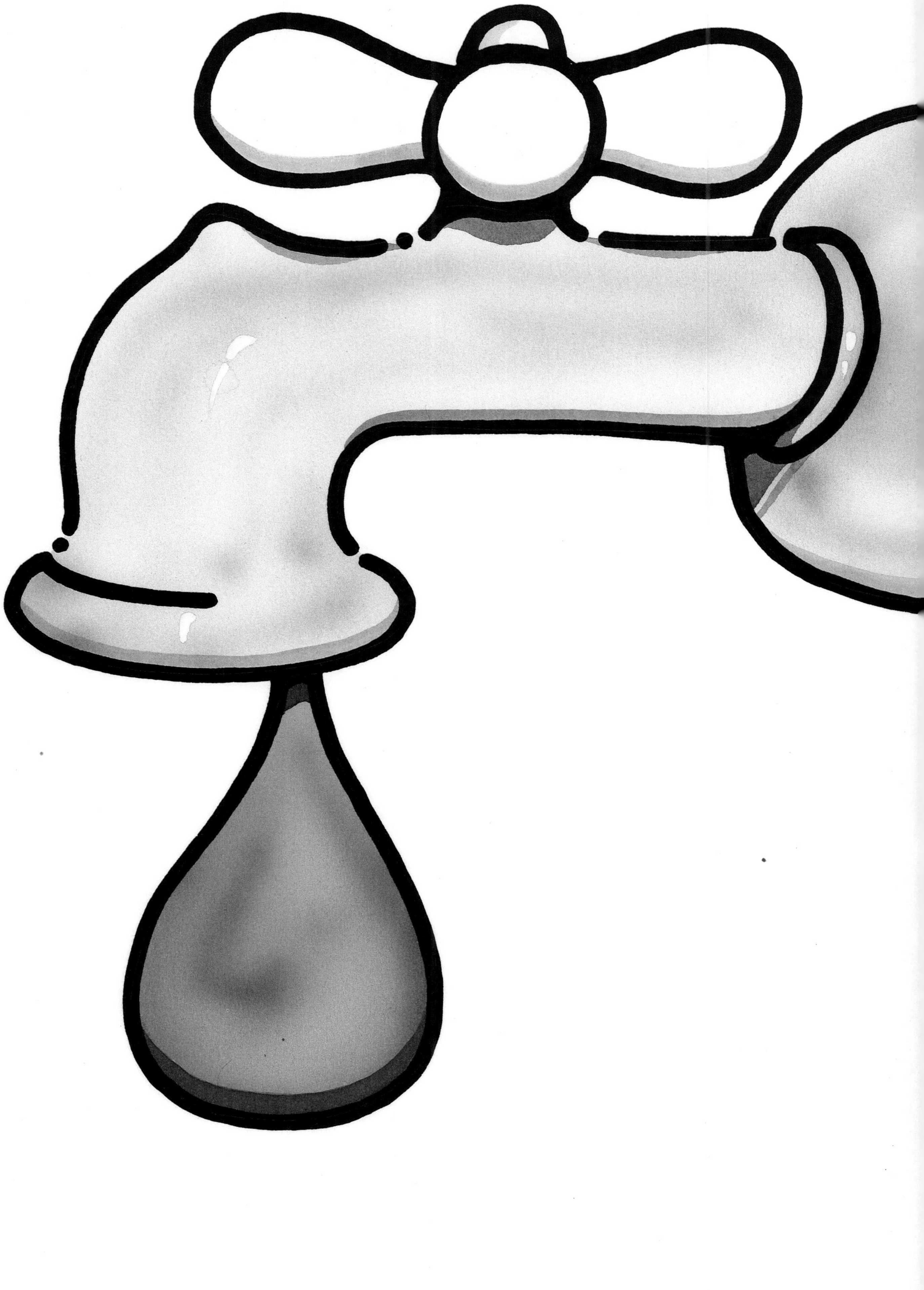

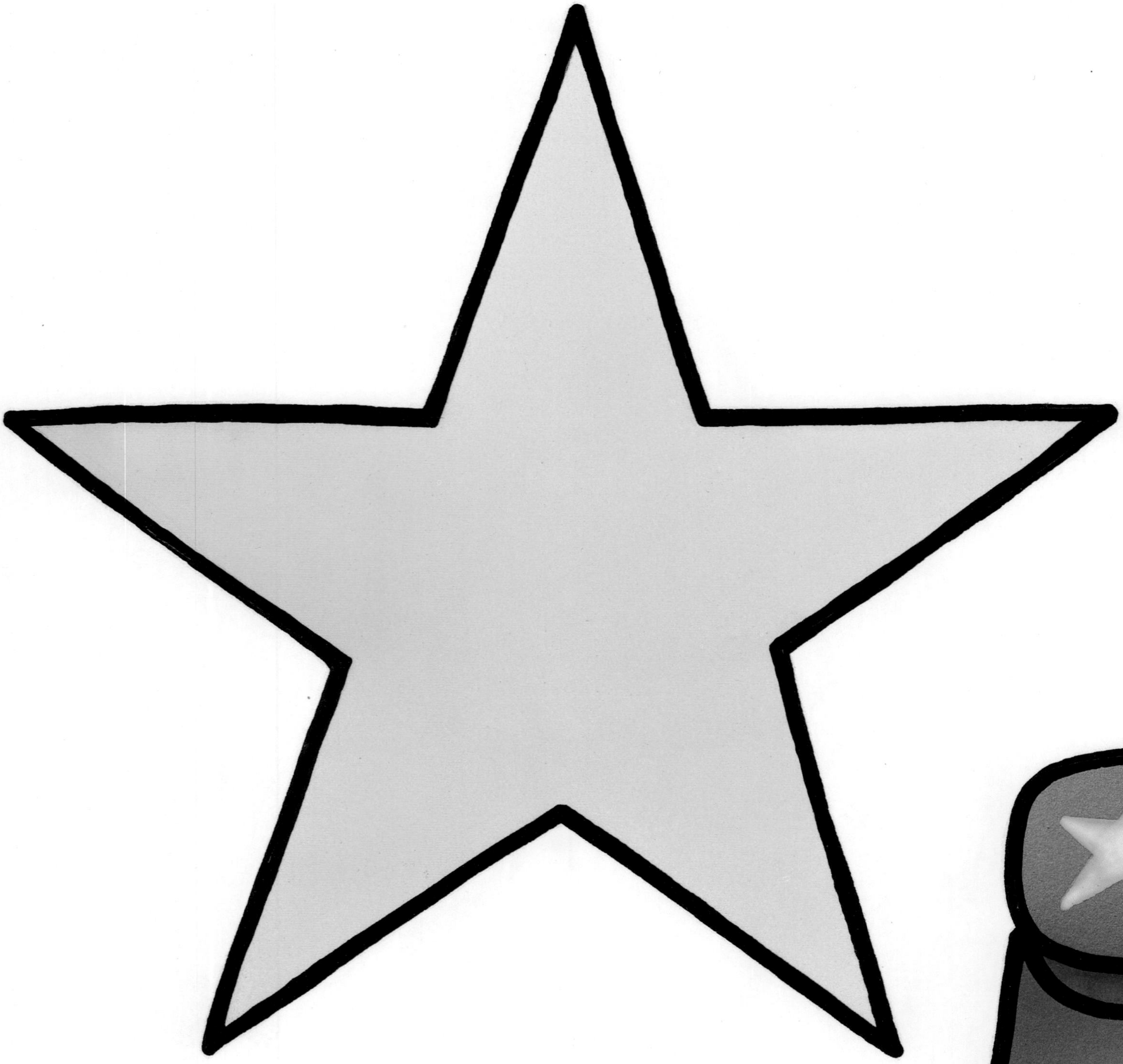

STAR

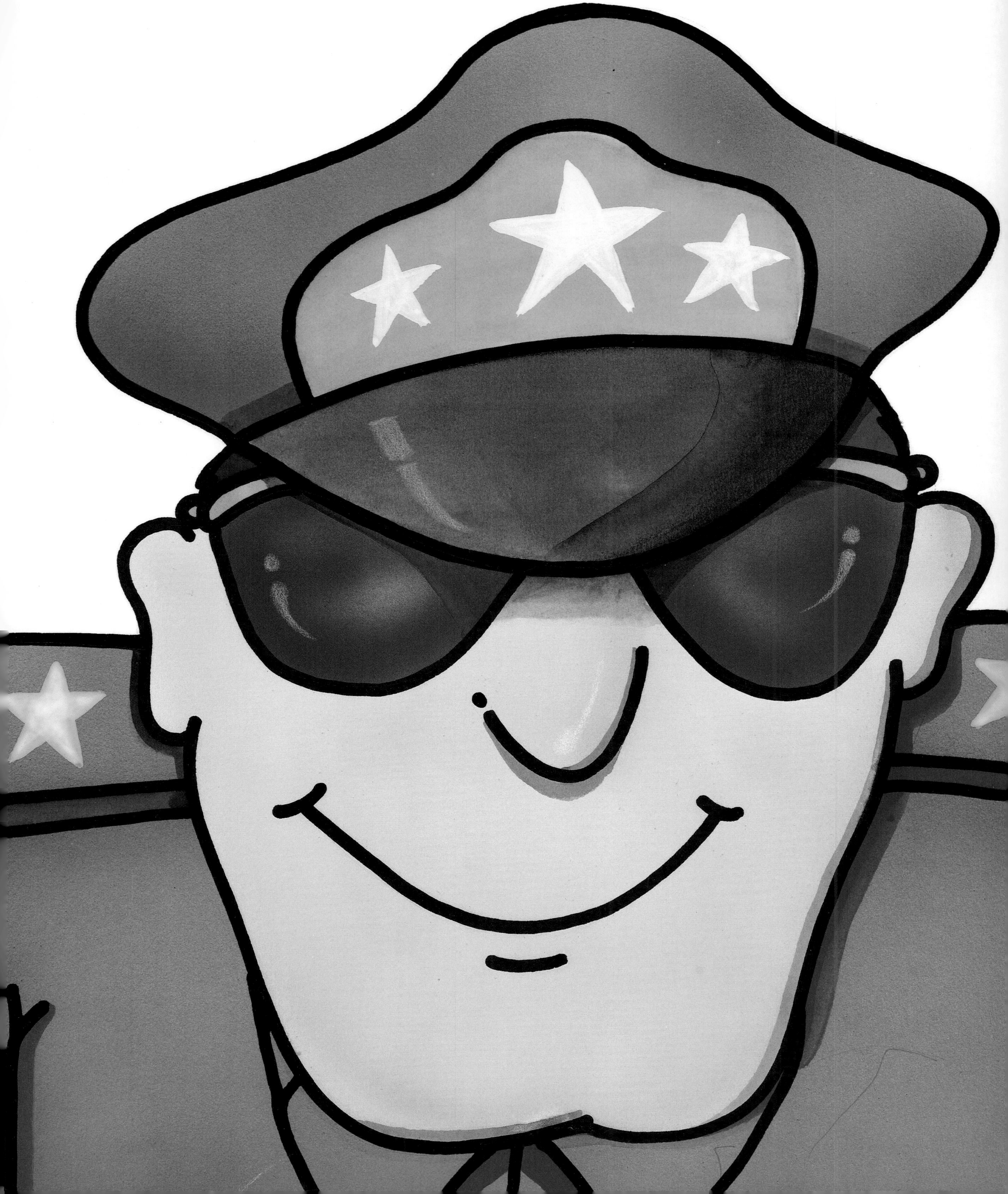

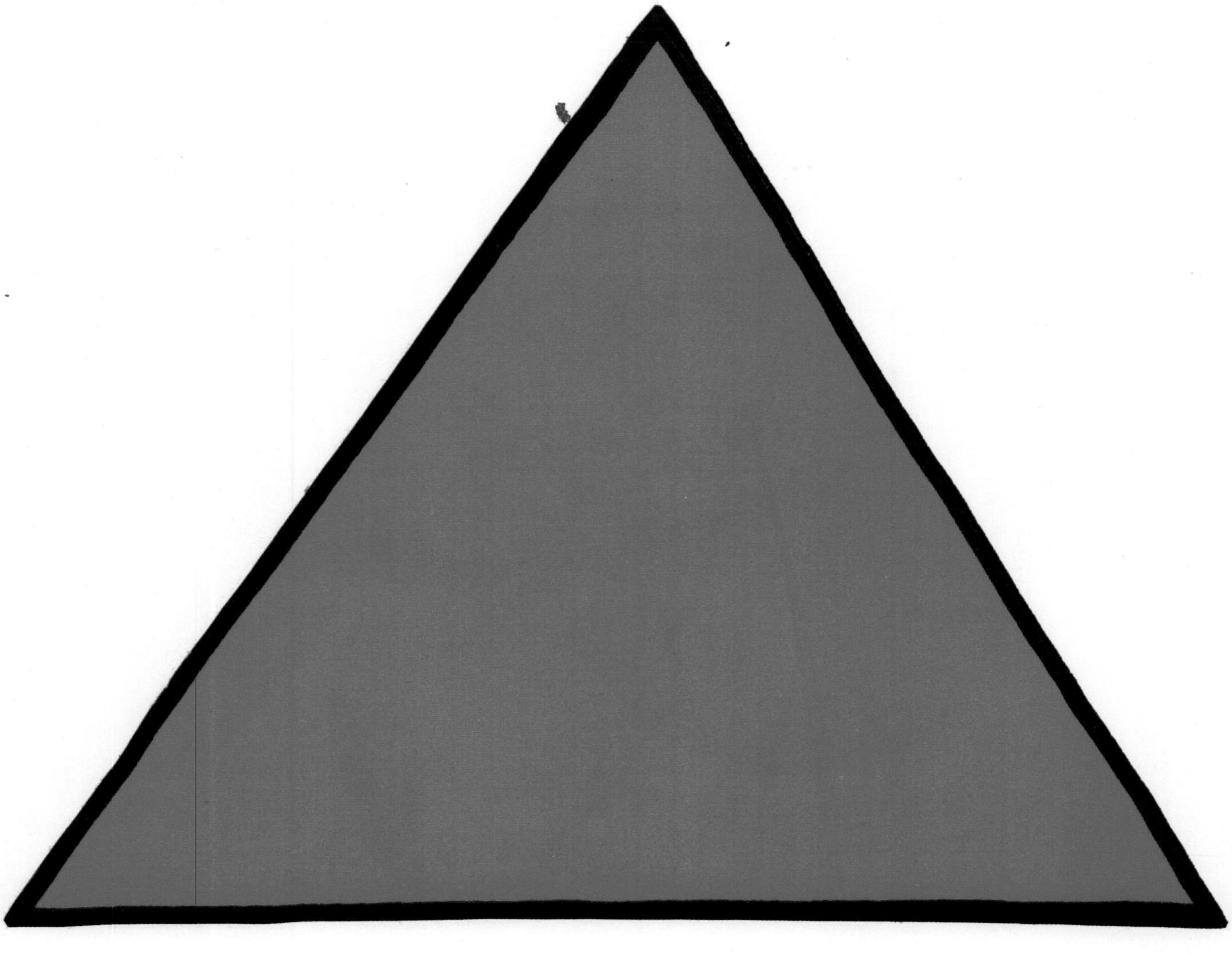

TRIANGLE

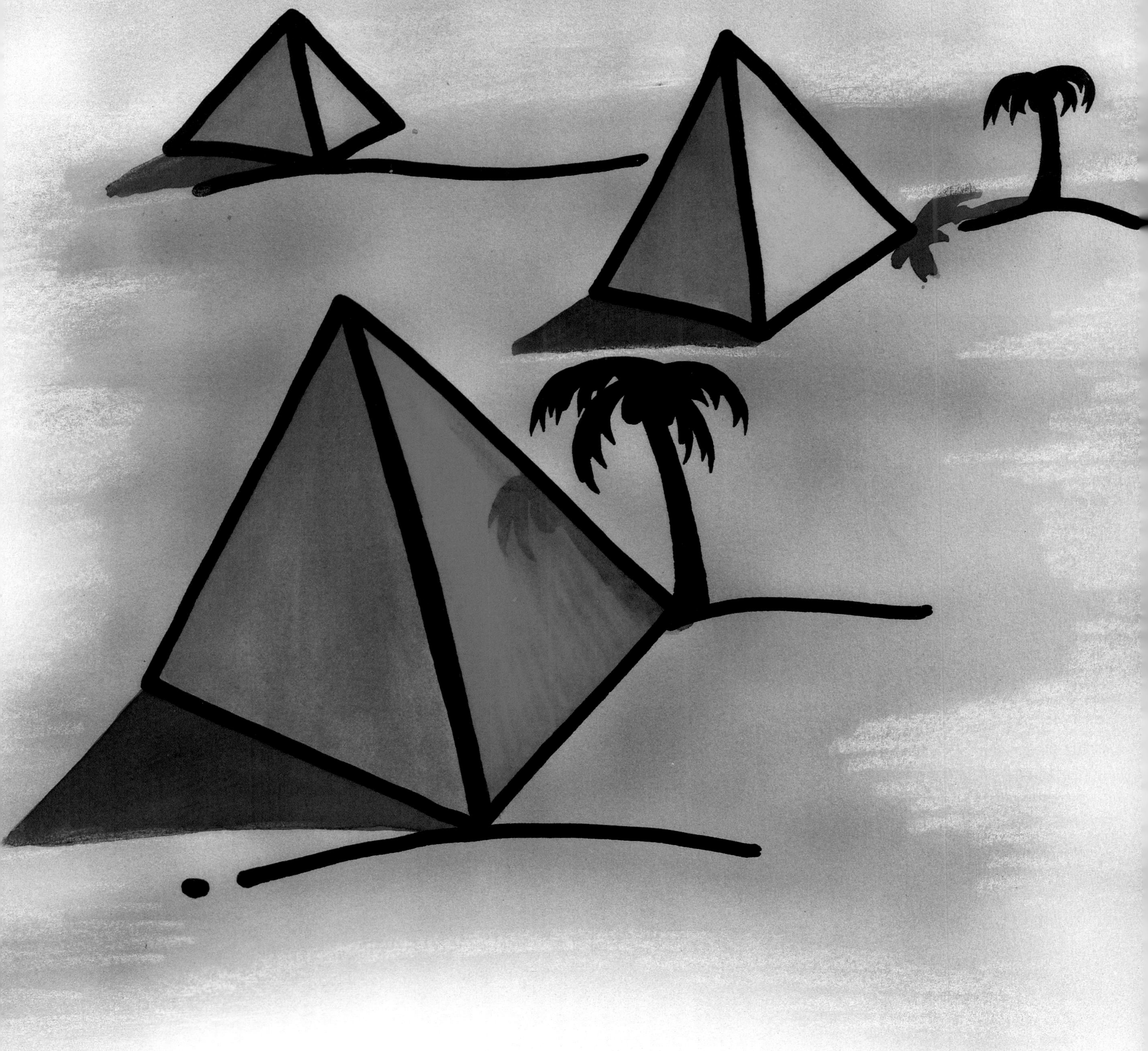

HEART

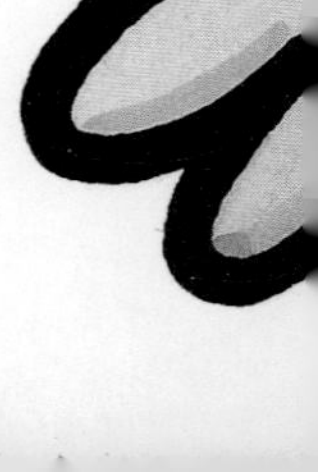

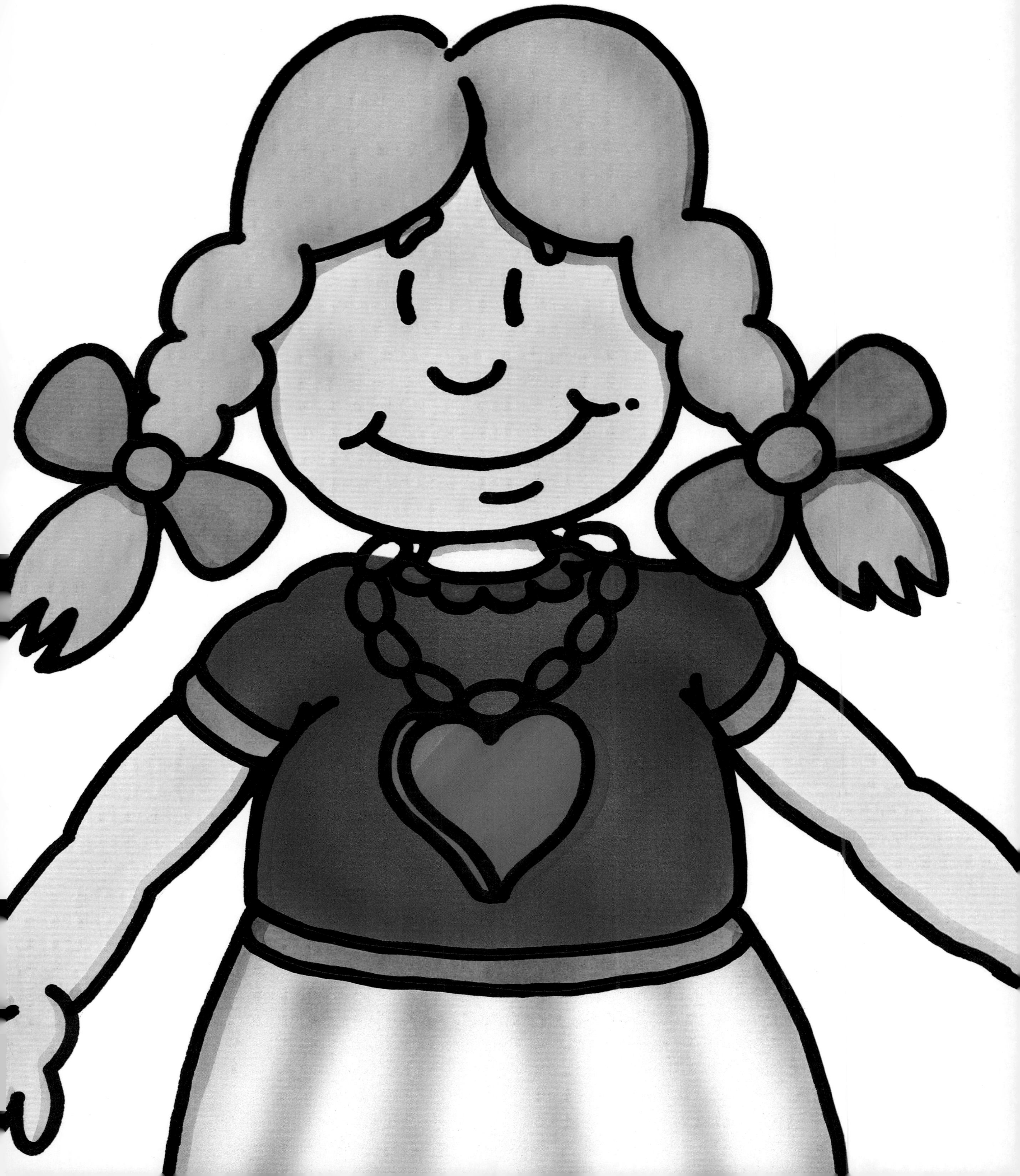

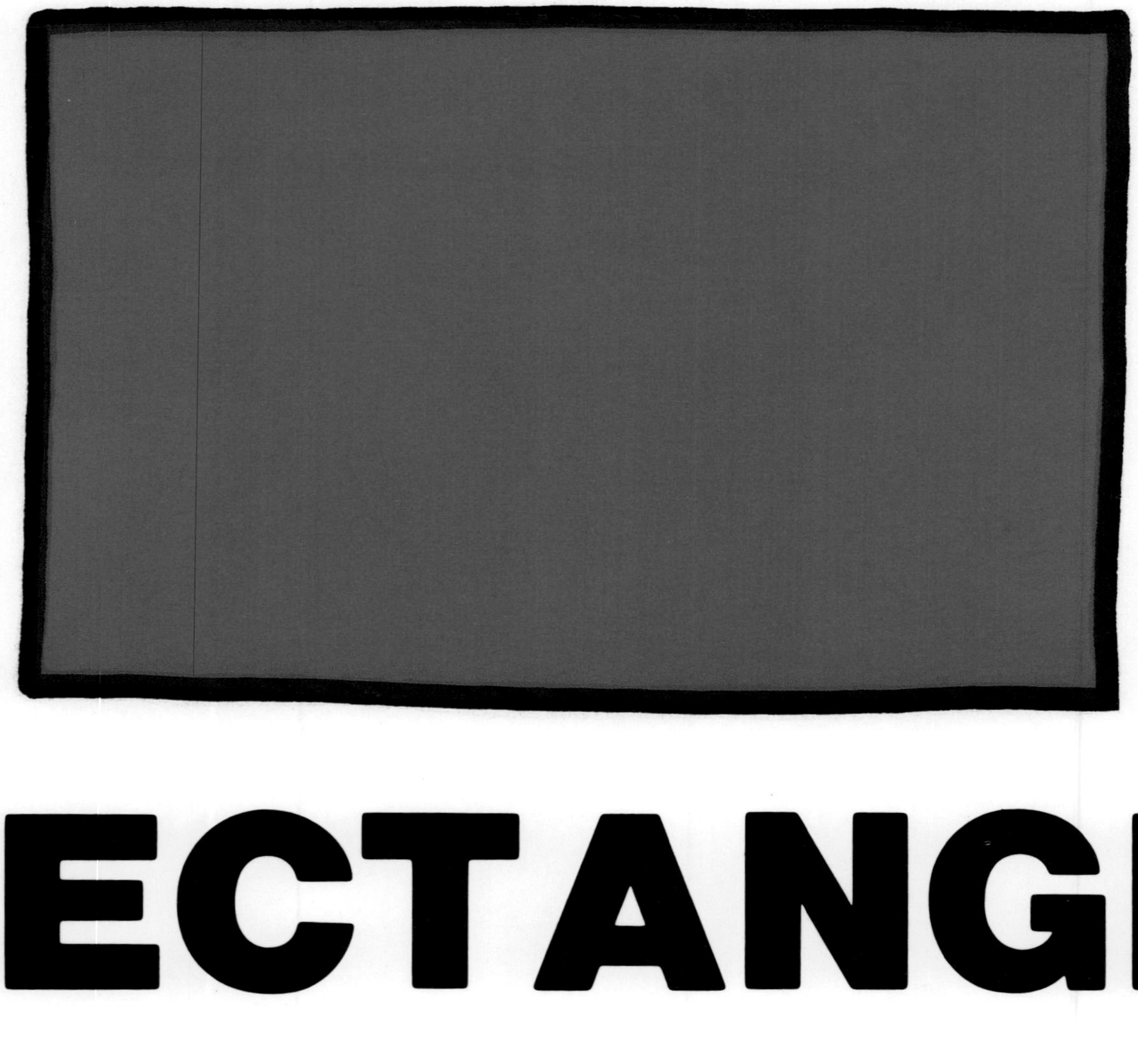

RECTANGLE

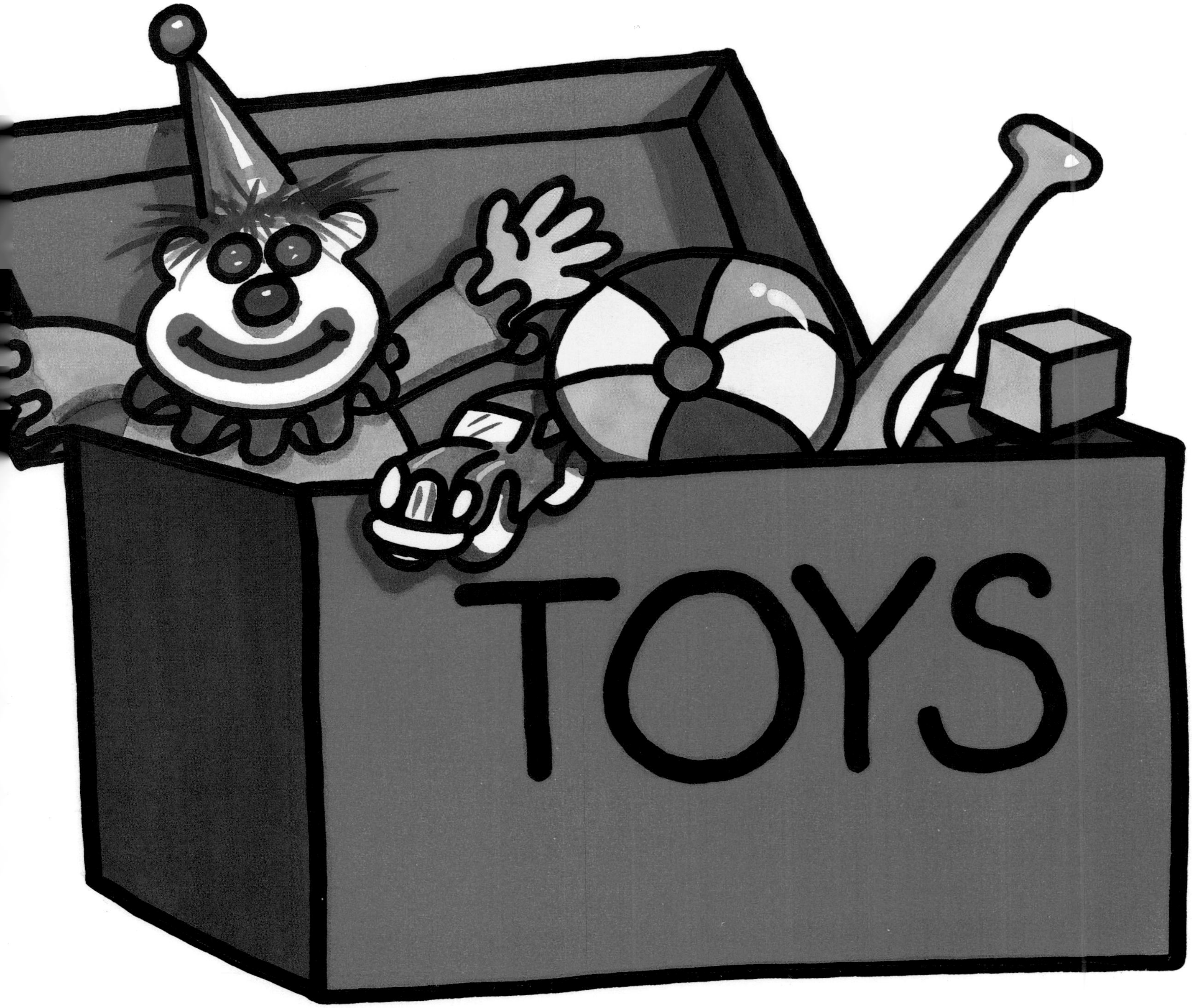
TOYS

CYLINDER

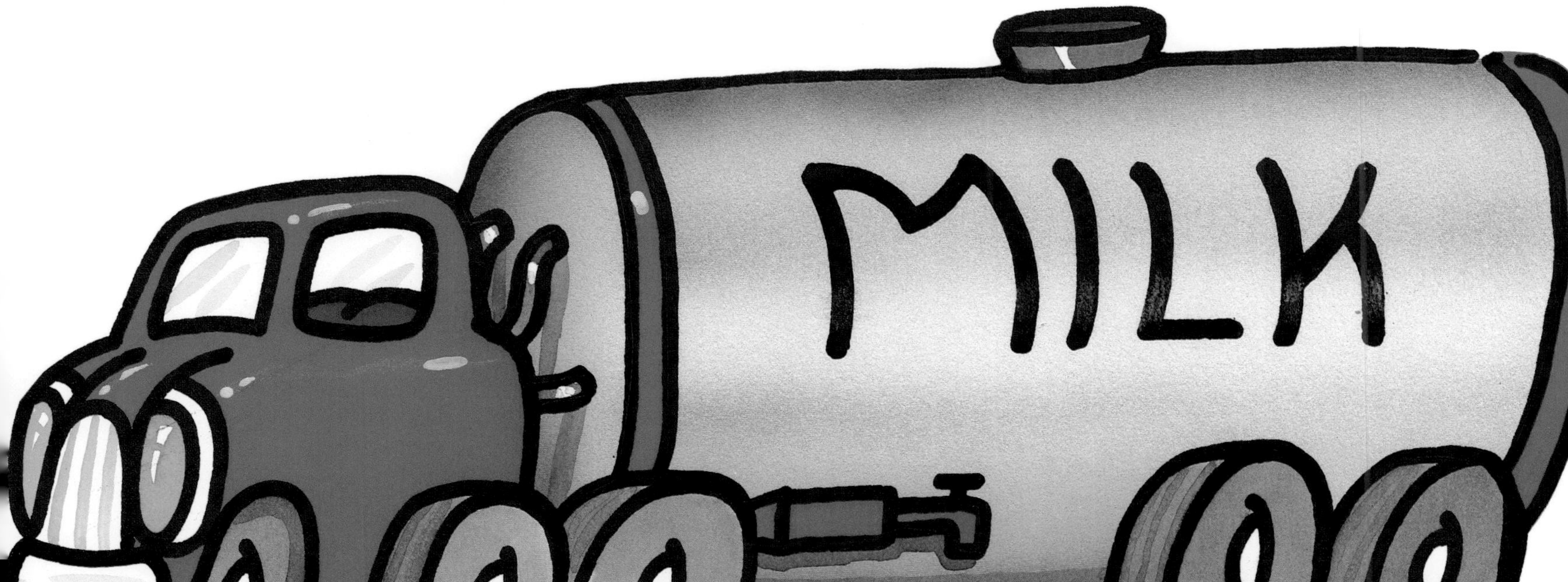
MILK

OVAL

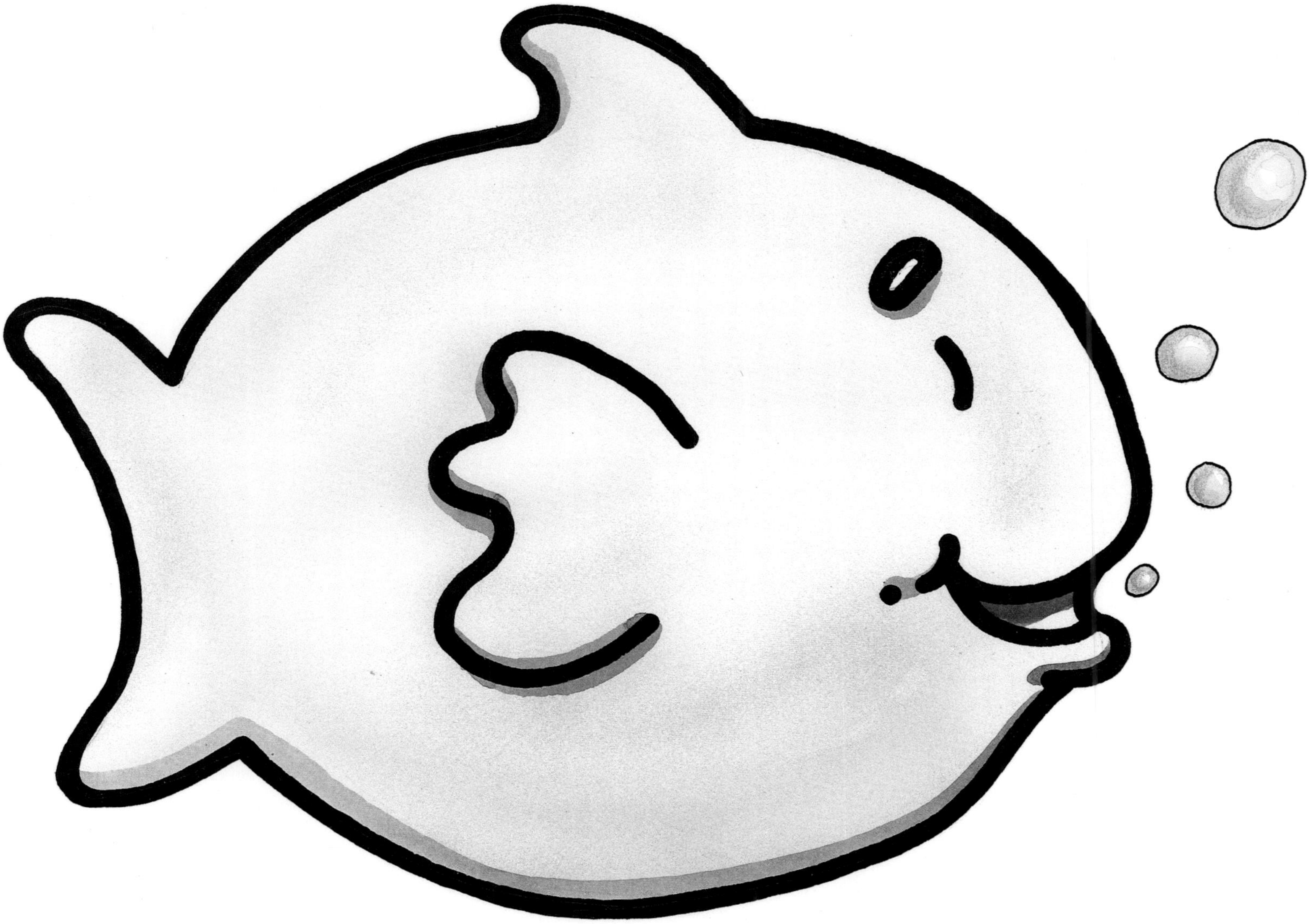

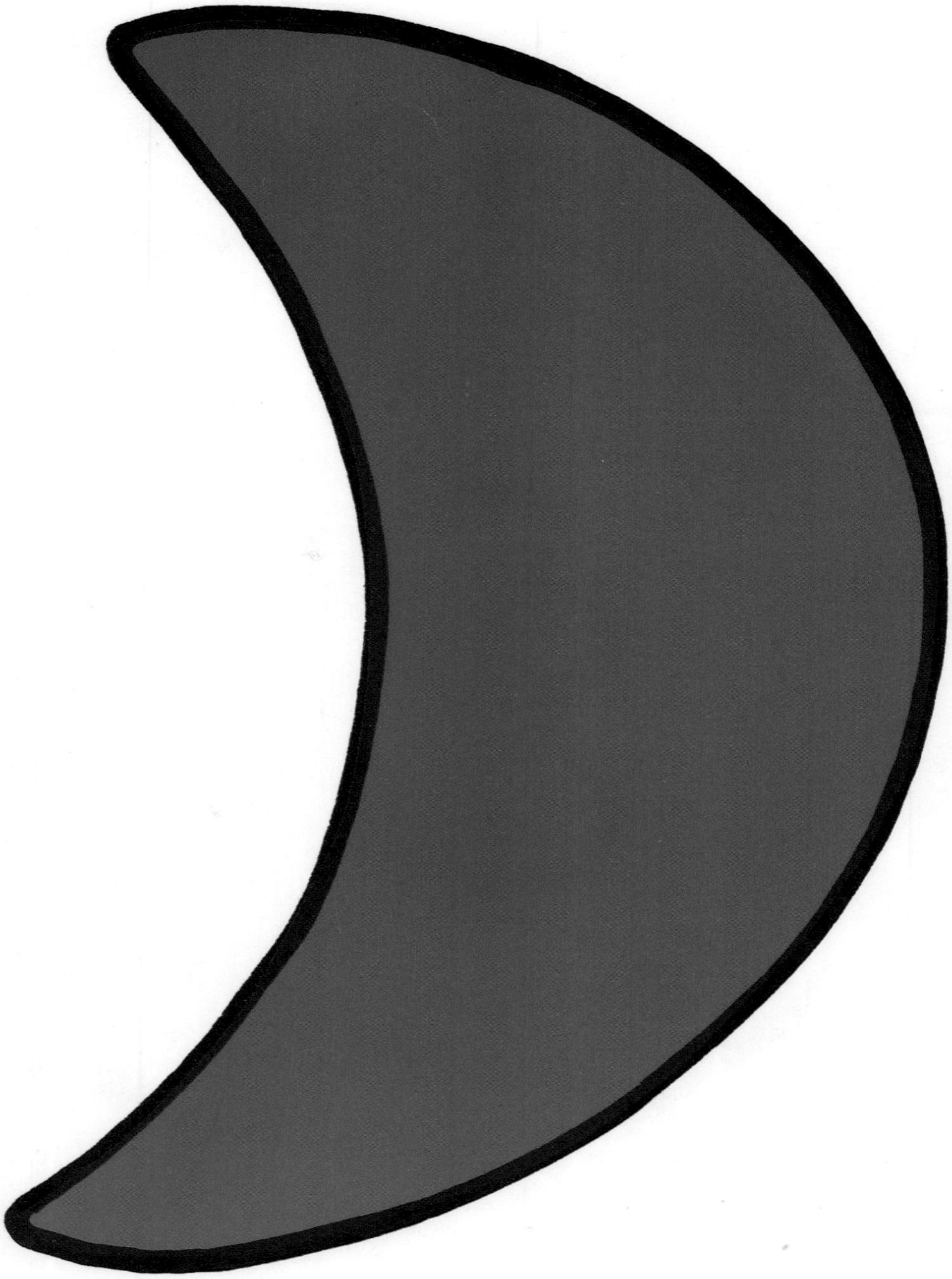

HALF MOON